TACKLING LOVE & CO.

HYMNS OF DESIRE

NEHA SHARMA JHA

Copyright © Neha Sharma Jha
All Rights Reserved.

This book has been published with all efforts taken to make the material error-free after the consent of the author. However, the author and the publisher do not assume and hereby disclaim any liability to any party for any loss, damage, or disruption caused by errors or omissions, whether such errors or omissions result from negligence, accident, or any other cause.

While every effort has been made to avoid any mistake or omission, this publication is being sold on the condition and understanding that neither the author nor the publishers or printers would be liable in any manner to any person by reason of any mistake or omission in this publication or for any action taken or omitted to be taken or advice rendered or accepted on the basis of this work. For any defect in printing or binding the publishers will be liable only to replace the defective copy by another copy of this work then available.

Dedicated to thoughts, which like a blessing, add meaning to my existence.

Thanks to my husband who is another name for blessing and truly a better half.

I owe my strength and courage to him. Also, my little bundle of joy adds perspective and peace to my life. Heartfelt thanks to my sister and parents who never give up on me.

Contents

Contents

1. Shakuntalam

Dazzling like sun
All night
Tired at dawn
She waned
She could
For she was moon
She was not in the mood
Shakuntalam of the streets
Waxed to please
Resolved to wane
Smirked Simone

2. Ravana

Don't talk to her about love
You don't know what it is
When you say barberry, it is raspberry,
No.
Barbarous.
When she says barberry, It is.
The farthest head
Hanging at the edge
Told *Ravana*
You might have heard it too
But ignorance is jaded bliss.
Applauded Tyranny
Where the sun never sets

3. Maneka

I like you, It is not enough
You have questions, I have answers too
To the questions, you have not asked
I am empty, No, I didn't say lonely
Tonight, I like you
Vishwamitra wasn't swayed, He was intrigued
A prolific passion, Quite a sight
Invoking in sight, An insight
Maneka merely inspired
Penance of desire, Dwells in acceptance
Combat is wearisome
Without a cause, mused King Jr.

4. Radha

Wall is bustling, It must be a war
Passing by. Should I open my door
And say Hi, Asked Radha to Krishna
No Krishna to Radha. Wife and Man. No. Man and Wife
A being in adulation of another
One and other, The other one, Another, Together
Are you alright? Yes, it is just the weather
Or is it the feather
Is the war within over? It has to be.
Where is peace? By invitation only
War and peace are lascivious
Lovers, that mustn't meet
To have one
Is to be without another
Leo might say on second thoughts

5. Dharmaraja

That tree
No, I would not call it a tree yet
It has a long way to go still
My balcony is not its beyond
There is possibility
For it is willing to withstand
The torments of that wind
No, it is not cruel
It is nature
All that is
Is amidst it
They are watching

6. Contd...

For the Fall
Of all hope
But those bunches
Of branches
What's holding them
The roots are in the grave
These offshoots are out
In the wind
Oh, out of my sight
I rush.It bent so low
Yet above the ground
Smaller stems cracked
There was still time
To transform

7. Contd...

But wind intervened
Uninvited, always does
A blizzard. It is January 15
Spring awaits, In a fortnight
To welcome the uprooted
Not to resurrect
That's up to me
Told *Dharmraja to the Dog*
At the gate between human and divine
But God is Dead, Friedrich said
Yes, I know short lived
In me
They said I killed him
Below

8. Contd...Concluding

They could be right
They were persuasive always are
I also didn't bother, Thinking for myself
Can be difficult, So I believed
You don't have to agree
With beliefs
I have thus set out, I am looking above
Dharmaraja looked at the Dog
I was human too beneath the name
You sometimes doubt who you are
And then the incredible
Better call it Dead, At least be sure of something
God is Dead, believe me said *Friedrich*
Dharmaraja started considering the proposition
Believing

9. Parshu

It is January
And it is raining in a desert
Yes, it is January again
And they are warring
Since inception
About what?
That's irrelevant
Then What for?
Nobody
Who is nobody?
Oh, it is somebody

10. Contd...

Is it someone known?
Known to me
Unfamiliar to you
How can that be?
And the war began
Again.
This time only *Parshu*
Ram was severed.
The mighty Parshu
Raged, unabated, unabashed
Leaped from behind
There were wars ahead

11. Draupadi

I am married
To my desire
But in solitude I meet
A few desires who are not
Married to me
Coiled *Draupadi*, coyly
Lawrence would agree
So would Lady Chatterley

12. Meera

I searched for You
Enchanted
I was then,I still am now
Celestial, No.Why do you always
Associate longing, With ethereal
My yearning is corporeal
Why, isn't in that a real too
Subdued.
I never said that I want you
I searched for you.
Period.
Meera was lost
In translation
She was inferred incessantly
Not once asked
Thus, laughed Medusa
Without asking

13. The Goga

I am having
an affair
It would be cruel
Not to have one
He knows it
My ineffable joy, He can't find it
For how anyone can
Find a thought
Gogaji, like you
A powerful thought
Slithering and hissing
Of course, said Oscar
I am wild

14. Sagarmanthan

I lie
Many times
How else should I talk
To you
My truth is
For the one
I am married to
Just as so
I don't lose sight
Of my other side
I practice lying
With you

15. Contd...

You don't believe me
You laugh at my lies
They come easily to you
You speak
Your truth with me
But how do you know my lies
We know
What we have known
Are you guarding your other side too
By lying to the one you are married to
Sagarmanthan.
Holding the Naga
Opposites, Yet holding the Naga
In the lightness of being, Distant thus bearable
Milan shakes his head in disdain
Appalled at adaptations

16. Takshak

I don't think of you, At bedtime
Lest you trespass, In my dream
And I speak your name in real
You, not You, I
Will be revealed
Revelations are not comforting
The claimants of visions
Have created crying
I am not one of them
I don't claim to reclaim
Somethings are best left unveiled
I wake up to myself
When you rest in peace in me.
Takshak thus listened
Coiled and waited
Awakened by Karma, not his own
The arch enemy of reason
Soon to be bitten by his feeling
Aghast, *Plutarch*

17. Jatayu

At least I should know whom I am talking to

I am wary of knowing everything, Isn't the unknown captivating

Absolute knowledge, overheard, absolute ignorance

Don't wait for the whistle

To blow for the

Race must stop

Intuitively

Let's start again but this time

Let's not follow

Lead.

Jatayu.

Become the path

Not succumb like Faustus

To foibles

Mourned, Mephistopheles

18. Narasimha

Walking together
Has been chaotic
I read headlines.
How about we walk alone
Let's not involve
First Evolve.
Soar above and beyond
The trivial
You don't know what is trivial?
Cruelty?
No
Violence.Power. Greed?
No

19. Contd...

Subservience? Not that too.
You enlist the consequences
Not the cause
Trivial is the thought
That provokes consequences
That which is not full
Is trivial
What if left unattended. Outlived.
Reasonable madness
Madness is captivating.Always ready
Agreed *Narasimha*
Of beings in being
A being in beings

20. Prakrti

I am waiting
So are you
It is a teasing
I know
So do you.
The edge of my toe tingles
In anticipation
Your neuron is mingling too
Knowing we indulge
In yearning
What is it?
Prakrti.

21. Narada

I don't drink
It has reputation to
Hither
I have a tendency
To thither
For I am intoxicated
In my well
Narada
Wasn't the greatest
Of all for *Narayana*
Maya sustains
Narayana overrules
Fair judgements but life
is unfair. What's wrong with unfair? Unfair isn't colorless.

22. Maya

I don't talk to you
Everyday
Lest you become a ritual
And I a devotee
I am devoid of devotion
Not of desire
For it is not perpetual
It is imprudent
Real
And that's where I can be
In *Maya* it can be too
The real manifests
Virtual reality

23. Raas Leela

I don't like metamorphosis
It grieves the essential
But doesn't offer it
There there,Keats offered solace
Beauty is everlasting joy
Dancing and twirling
Ras Leela.
Cosmic Ras.
In you and me
Nowhere in sight,
Presence
Leela behind the eyes
In every breath of space

24. Indra

The other day
He asked whether he ever
Asked me to change
If I accept him as he expects me to be
Then that's a change for me
And I thought, there is none
As troubled as me,akin to me
Indra smiled.

25. Brahma

It doesn't come easy you
Know, the forgetting
I have to remember
A lot, to forget
It is not easy
To forget yourself
And be left with You
From *Brahma's* mankind
Came a wailing kind

26. Suras &Asuras

War they say is brutal
Nay, I say
Love is
War ends
Love lasts
Suras and Asuras yet again agreed with
The *Almighty*
I am All, smirked Suras
But I am Mighty, Asuras laughed off
I am neither
Both agreed again.
With whatever

27. Krishna

Talk to me about
The beginning
Everyone else is
Talking about the end
Let's talk about the proximity
That never ends
Urged *Krishna*
Come again, I said.

28. Durga

You said that you
Love me
Then bring me
Down from your imagination
Love my reality
Durga was displeased
By the worship
Shakti was debarred
The devotee argued, I worship
In thee, that which pleases me
Please yourself
Know thyself

29. Returning Ravana

I am not absconding
It is my thoughts
Fleeting desire
Not undesirable
But undesired
Willfully
I want to keep my desire
Unfulfilled
Thus, a desire
Like you
Distant
When the time comes
I shall scheme and invite you
Thought *Ravana*
Until then take me lightly

30. AdiShakti

There is nothing between us
I insist
Except a moment
Of being beheld
Doing nothing
Merely engaged
In an unflinching gaze
From *ShivParvati*
To *UmaShankar*
And so existed
SitaRam
Thus followed *RadheShyam*

31. Sita

How do you annul
The all pervasive
There is no relationship of sorts
No presence
Absence though attends memory
Frequently.Singularly
Multiplying continuously
That never were
In the world
But there is a world in me
Nothing ends there
So spoke *Sita*,
Ashoka stood
Silent.Listening.
She had more to say
But the desire
That precedes utterance
Had embarked from afar

32. Narayana

I look at you
It is a relationship
I see others
Watching each other
I don't see them looking
But they know each other
So, they say.
Is it true?
How can I know you?
Without looking at you?
Just as Narayana does
How can a Nar become Narayana
Can it not?
It can
It hasn't yet.

33. ArdhNarishwar

He knows what she
Has told
He doesn't know much
He says, is it necessary to know it all?
The rise and the fall?
I wonder.
He could be right.
She didn't tell
He knows what she has told.
ArdhNarishwar knows it all?
The zenith and nadir of it all

34. Kandarpa

There is more to love
Then what meets the eye
Nay the soul, nay the inward
Aye, a wilderness
A sway, A madness bereft of a justify
An impulse, A poise
To veil a moment
In a day
A demeanor to
Conceal
A night
Yet continue
A love you chose
And gaze when love chooses you
Love, as you find it, as it does when it finds you, dazzling *Kandarpa*

35. Mahabharata

My shadow is long
Soaked in scintillations
Silently soaking me
I can see my silhouette
I have rather broad shoulders
Hunched
I prefer my dos
Over the don'ts
I've always had long hair
Mostly untied
Up to my lower back
I can't see my back
Sometimes I can't see my face
My shadow hides my face

36. Mahabharata contd...

My cashmere is easy going
slipping
touching my shoulder
splitting it in smile
my hair tingles it
Repeatedly
Unasked, uninvited
But not undesired
Pepper is salting my hair
But my shadow is black
I stand out in it
Said *Sati*, the infinite *Shakti*
It is today, begin, affirm, acknowledge
Echoed the craft of *Mary*.

37. Mahabharata continues

I need something
To keep going
It can't be love
I will return
I had embarked
As you know
But your thoughts
Walked along
I have returned
You look alarmed,
I never said
I would be the same.
Mahabharata is unfazed
The warriors too remain enraged
Nothing changes but us
Only we can
With love
By Love
For Love. Nor for the Love of. Not for the Love of.